T0317191

THE DEEP
HEART'S CORE
IS A SUITCASE

The publication of this book is supported by a grant
from the Eric Mathieu King Fund of The Academy of American Poets

The New Issues Press Poetry Series

Editor   Herbert Scott

Advisory Editors   Nancy Eimers
                            Mark Halliday
                            William Olsen
                            J. Allyn Rosser

Assistant to the Editor   Rebecca Beech

Fiscal Officers   Michele McLaughlin
                            Marilyn Rowe

The editors wish to thank Douglas Ferraro for his essential
support in the establishment of this series.

The New Issues Press Poetry Series is sponsored by
The College of Arts and Sciences, Western Michigan University,
Kalamazoo, Michigan 49008.

The publication of this book is supported by the Arts Council of
Greater Kalamazoo through a program of The Michigan Council
for the Arts and Cultural Affairs.

ISBN: 0-932826-46-6 (casebound)
          0-932826-47-4 (softbound)

Library of Congress Cataloging-in-Publication Data:
Fishman, Lisa, 1966–
The Deep Heart's Core is a Suitcase / Lisa Fishman
Library of Congress Catalog Card Number 96-69693

Design   Tricia Hennessy and Brian Edlefson
Production   Paul Sizer
                 The Design Center, Department of Art
                 Western Michigan University
Printing   Bookcrafters, Chelsea, Michigan

THE DEEP
HEART'S CORE
IS A SUITCASE

LISA
FISHMAN

FOREWORD BY WILLIAM OLSEN

New Issues Press

WESTERN MICHIGAN UNIVERSITY

for Holly

Contents

II Deceptive Country

III Night Skiing

Foreword

The shape-shifting realms of longing are fitful setting for local genius. But here, in Lisa Fishman's beautiful first collection of poems, is where for the love of the world we find ourselves. As a reader, I could say I see in these poems a devotion approaching to love, if love ever stayed still enough to take a linguistic reading of. The poet sees much more, though. There's possibly no harder stance for the young poet to take up than one of love and longing— Richard Hugo used to adjure his students to put off writing their first love poem until they were fifty—but there is no more tempting subject either, and Lisa Fishman is not a poet who contents herself to live out as truth the easy injunctions from the Fathers or the Mothers. Besides, as she writes in "V's Farmhouse," "no one ever died of desire." That's a witty line. It's a line that puts the brakes on the aesthetics of death-wish Romance; and, like all of Fishman's effortless seeming assertions, it feels thought out and lived in. As wit goes, and in poetry it too often goes fast and furious and blind, this line has, to quote another father, a self-appointed one, T.S. Eliot, a "tough reasonableness beneath the lyric grace."

Fishman's poems get at their hard subjects and their scarcely inhabitable places by owning up to their own loves, and their duplicities, and their split-second sidetrackings. Through intelligence, unashamed, unnerved intelligence— she is a new metaphysical poet, one thoroughly conversant in the theory of our time—and through a responsive pliant syntax that never quite breaks. Her poems are tough reeds in the purgatorial wind. There is a growing number of young poets who have figured a way out of the purportedly image-based, purportedly plain speech, purportedly sincerist poetry of a few decades ago, and that's a good thing, as there's always room in Parnassus for dazzle and flair and smart talk. And for all the puritanical mispractices of a new aesthetic correctness, it is also about time that we started distrusting the colonizing impulses of our language. But what too often happens out of collective wisdom is a poetry that, in the hopes of righting itself, goes so far into its prospectus that it begins to mistake its intentions for moral accomplishments, and then it begins to condescend to its own past. So the rich dialogue of poetry becomes reduced to a dialogue of art with art, and we end up in that place below purgatory that George Oppen calls "the no world of artyness." Yet this is a rich time for poetry, too: witness, here is one more unsettled traveler.

Unsettled in fact, in mind and in heart. Fishman's poems seem to have endless riches and eccentric offerings at their reach. Probably there is a quality in any successful poem that always seems found, its poet gift-ed by its offerings by being given over to them, and Fishman's poems have more than their share of the glories of experience. Which is to say they have very little to count on, yet very much to take account of: they have a speaker whose father sends her a third of his winnings and comes home "carrying all that money/ that never even felt like his." They have visits home at summer and a hammock that blows like "a little boat/ of ropes in the wind." A lover "pissing a long arc into the sumac and Queen Anne's lace" who "didn't even have to leave the room." They keep their humor in their real travels to the inextricably mixed and constantly re-evolving frontier lands of the global culture, as to an Italy where "In Rome a priest named Valdimar pronounced my name in Portuguese." They have a speaker driving closer and closer to home but not so close as all that: "I'm driving home through Couer d'Alene, the road like a waltz lurching forward on its one bad knee." They have, constellating around their poet, fellow travelers to equally deceptive, equally longed-after realms, as a Major General one brief century away from us who finds his sole bearings in his journal, in which he writes, just like one of us moderns might, "As the sun rose today I looked out upon—what shall I say, the lake?"

And at bottom, in the journeys of these poems charged by the prospect of getting somewhere, Fishman acknowledges what's at stake, what the real cost is—that the danger of being lost is losing a sense of where we once were, which is also where we are, and which to see long enough to get into words takes a steady eye, and not just an art rising from the ashes of a junked tradition, but a self-critical art.

Fishman's poems offer many pleasures, and if these pleasures prove sometimes to be difficult ones, this is only because Fishman forces her art out into the neglected world where difficulties really begin. Yet these are also internal, tremendously internal poems. Internality in poetry often turns out to be the vanishing point of the world, but not in these poems. Their interests— the poet's fractured family, her distant relations, saints and artist-saints including Stravinsky and the great Czech photographer Josef Sudek, the desert reaches of Utah, the boggy waterlands of Michigan—are only as diffuse as human curiosity at its most engaged is diffuse. So the poems are true, inwardly focused, but outwardly transfixed. The urgency of their thoughtliness suggests that whatever current comforts of theory we affix ourselves to, theory is not the to-die-for of intelligence but the dream that precedes the to-live-for of reality. In short these poems try only anything that works, including poetry:

> It is to figures of speech that we return.
> My heart is on fire, we say
> or, her love rides like the wind.
> Do we seek exactitude, or the rain
> to sail its ships down our backs?

It is wondrous that these poems so often find, in their moments of truest perplexity, ecstatic outreach. Fishman may be dissatisfied with her art, but she is never dismissive, never coy; and when she allows herself transport, it is transport back to somewhere just as needful of our care as the last poor place we found ourselves. Here are the last stanzas of "Ave Maria," a "love" poem—a poem that spans the natural world and contemporaneity and a not-so-distant time of medieval monks in prayer. It is a poem that in its crosscuts from one dark age to the next bids a wary invitation to the future, tendering its numbered desires as echoes of innumerable continuities:

> The car glides like an egg through the centuries falling around it,
>
> but the voices merge, singing.
> It's 1297. Stone gates,
>
> cobblestone. Where shall we lay our weary heads
> if the story holds them together like peas in a pod,
>
> like a hand in a glove: will they ever stop singing,
> is there world without end?
>
> Salt streaks the car and a mule deer waits for the lights
> to stop blinding. (*It's not that I want to leave—*)
>
> But what they are singing is not about love.
> It's about wanting the story, driving all night
>
> and waiting for someone
> to say, *that man*
>
> or, *this woman*
> *is mine.*

Any expectation we have of possessing the desired is, alas, as these last lines sing without disguise, going to get us into trouble. Trouble that this poet gets beyond only by passing through it, to something like understanding. That something is all there is, and it—and this fine debut—is rare passage, indeed.

William Olsen

Acknowledgments

Grateful acknowledgment is made to the editors of the following publications where these poems first appeared:

Alaska Quarterly Review: "Mary's Angel," "Wood Heat"

The Antioch Review: "The Fire of Love," "Leelanau County"

Hayden's Ferry Review: "The Hills Have Gone Into the Country"

Louisiana Literature: "Night Skiing," "Tracks"

Maryland Poetry Review: "Ave Maria"

National Poetry Competition Awards Annual:
"In the Absence of Field Guides"

Poetry Northwest: "Three-Quarter Moon"

Roberts Writing Awards Annual: "Scavengers"

The Wallace Stevens Journal: "Exchange"

Thanks to Catherine Kaikowska, Diane Wakoski, and William Olsen. Thanks also to Douglas Wolk, and deepest gratitude to Ron Dorr at James Madison College.

I Leelanau County

Proximity

*In heaven, the angels which burn most brightly in love
are nearest to God.*
                    —Richard Rolle, 1343

You say they're only in it
because they want to touch:
they burn
according to proximity—
Could it be so clear?

In heaven, the old desires
shoulder past the new ideas.
They declare themselves
in love.
We have not got names
for all of them.

They disappear
in their own burning.
See, they become
the fire.

The Fire of Love

I have too many prints unframed
but propped against the walls regardless.
Meant to remind me of the job of finishing,
they only sit for years as if no need for borders
or edges that confine. In "Twilight" a woman
whirls herself across a field
of bloodroot and anemone. She is all arms
and drapery, truly she is
not bound by gravity,
as if the purpling light unwrapped her
from clouds the viewer cannot see.
      It must have been like this
when Richard Rolle saw Christ descend, no colors
but shadows mountains took behind him—
At how this burning in my soul leapt up, he said;
the clouds coming in over the canyon
cannot be the same
as the colors I name them by: light
blue, pink-streaked, they're not the same
as those which she is flying through,
finely lined in antique-green.
The heat in which all darkness is consumed
has no place except within the curve
of her elbows, wrapped around her body
to keep her warm or to propel her,
driving her forward though her feet tip up
as if her speed surprises even her.
      He wanted to be lifted up
in that lovely burning fire, wanted all his flesh
consumed: bone, sinew, marrow,
these are the things of the world but look
how she uses her thighs, presses
into them, the muscle
wanton beauty is. It forces her
through anemone and all desire

to remain unharmed. *Who is there who could bear for long*
her opening
       her arms and letting go
the darkness we can see held in
between such folds of drapery and the shadows
entangled in her scarves in flight.
He must too have loved
the unraveling dusk and grey-
green tilt of the bloodroot—
how could he not? His heart,
he said, was burning—call it Christ, call it
inordinate; other people love *temporal things*
more than eternity. Never wanting
what they wanted, how then could he
name it: *and their hearts are entirely ravished away.*

Tracks

algebra: from al-jabr, "reunion of broken parts"

All the light came down like algebra.
So it was when everything that fell could see itself:
an etymology of green, then, in a green world
where loss is everything we have. And wanting, somehow,
to get back in. On County Road 669,
coming home with all our laundry
behind us in the pick-up truck, it sometimes came unbundled
and flew off, still warm
from the dryer. But if the clothing could be seen—
my sister's bright red turtleneck—
we'd turn around to get it.
My mother told me order's an illusion
when I couldn't make my bed exactly right.
The untucked corners could not please me, nor explain
the hills when everything even the light is leaving
and the mist is elegy to what was solid.
If we could say the garden's a reunion
of calla lilies, pigeonberry, and yellow wild
indigo, do we then reclaim
everything we've given up—the story problems taking leave
like sheets and nightgowns newly cleaned and tumble-dried,
flying off behind the truck? The compass plant.
Silphium laciniatum. Is it this
that will find the way home? *Loves me, loves me not.*
Until they got it right. Until they want
what got away—*illusion, al-jabr,* the end
of all false starts to follow.

The Sisters

Simply, I smiled more
because I knew my sister
with almond eyes and darker hair
was Beauty's child, truly. She
kept her mouth closed. My teeth
were straight. This is the edge
of the photograph and this
is the younger sister, twisting her hands
while I posed in the center, head thrown back,
hand on hip. You cannot see her
stuttering, how she couldn't
get a sentence out, how I convinced her
I could make her smaller
with the motion of my hands just so,
until she came to be
invisible. At night we shared my double bed
so we could talk more easily than from across the room.
When we walk toward each other now,
everyone believes we're twins.
She knows me best because she knows my cruelty
did somehow make us allies, how I know
the curve of her back (whole nights
encircled around it), how we keep
each other visible, in each
reappearing another.

Leelanau County

In French I said my name was *Nadine*, in Spanish,
Rosalinda. What we want most to translate is ourselves.
Such as, *the pipes froze nightly*
in the farmhouse, and my mother kneeled under
the kitchen sink. She warmed them with a hairdryer
until water came out warm enough to take our makeup off.
Those days we wore "foundation," lined our eyes in black.
1980, cherry crops were hit by early freeze,
the farmers stayed out longer at the taverns. I'd be a virgin
for three more years; in nine a girl would be shot
in the high school parking lot. *He loved her so much*,
the headlines said
of the sixteen-year-old boyfriend
and, *she was killed but both were victims*.
       When languages were canceled,
we still used our foreign names,
appropriating beauty in the only way we knew.
The mirrors were sick with all desire
we poured into them, to look like *this*, like that.
We ate cold lunch in front of them
and threw the fattening bread away.
What we're left with are the names that still
sound pretty and the blood-
stained stones between the bleachers and the gravel lot.
       The black walnuts from the tree my sister
and I together could not wrap our arms around
stained our hands and stained the oak table
each Spring we sorted them for sale. How much could it matter
when she jabbed a pencil deep into my palm
and it bled all the way to the hospital?
No one said *crime of passion* and it wasn't. But when she had a hoof
imprinted on her face
after falling underneath the stallion, I was jealous. So many ways
to mar a body, as if what we're composed of

are the shapes borne into it, the losses. We wanted
to protect the table, we covered it
with newspaper. Our hands
stayed yellow-green for days.

Stone Silo, Wheeler Road

The blue chords of remembering
have nothing to do with us. In which
the hawk dips downward and its wing just brushes
white white leaves
of a tree in winter.
Snow's crusted on the ground, at night
all the stars in the world.
You must be looking down to see them.
You must change the way you see. We have not
so much we haven't lost—little longings and O a certain beauty—
but listen now to the scraping
of branches against themselves. It's the scraping of your feet
on ice-encrusted snow, and of wings
in the branch of a tree.
      You think one touch
can fasten you? One shoulder cupped in the palm,
the bones behind the shoulder—angelwings—
rising as if in flight or falling? If a stone
silo on a dirt road
appears, at night, larger than it is,
inside your voice will fall until it edges
out of hearing. Once a warbler flew around, seeming not to want
to come out of the open wall.
      I used to lie in the field and the wind
scraped me and the wheat at once. Imagine this wind
as steady, as *direction*
blowing over you: north, south, east and the hawk
flew west out of a tree. It was a branch across
her eye. Her, I, the field a dream of one wrong wing
closing ground beneath her feet.

Wager

My father, prospector and carpenter,
cleans hallways on the cusp
of Santa Anita, sends us racing
charts and when he wins,
sends each of us one third.
One summer we played slot machines,
looked for 3 bright oranges in a row.
Once, a hundred quarters clanked into the till:
bus fare, laundry, Friday nights at Pinball Pete's:
with luck I win free games
on the *Elvira* machine, all lights
and numbers flashing—it's then I think of my father,
how we cannot gather him up
from the casinos: not hungry,
no shoelaces, and carrying all that money
that never even felt like his.

Bequests from Grandparents Unknown

Clara, who undressed only in the dark,
cried when I was born. A girl, she said,
will have it hard.

I cannot really tell her story.
She wore the hats that Harry made.
She coughed up blood.

In Hebrew class my father
never knew what he was saying
so forbade me from Allegiance pledged in school.

The hides for all his father's hats had need
of being softened, as onions before roasting,
or rye crust rubbed with butter and with garlic.

I have only a word or two: menorah, Clara
lighting it. Tuberculosis, dying of it. I have
Harry Fishman's handedness. His fault, then,

kept in from recess? Construction paper
into flowers, couldn't cut
with scissors fumbling, nothing to show

for all my efforts, though I had the classroom
to myself, *to get it right*.
I'd like to hear him say believe no one

who says the left hand fails.
In Russia and in Montréal the white fur hats were larger
than loaves of round or braided *challah*.

Clara said the wind
off the St. Lawrence chills the city to its bones.
I'd like to hear him say believe me.

If you had kept the hats I made,
precisely cut and sewn,
I swear inside your head you'd never feel the cold.

The Autobiographer's Lament for a Landscape Unknown

I still wish to be beloved.
— A. M. R. Richards to her daughters, Boston, 1854

Girls now listen, you must divine the bees
buzzing in this other heart, where the Lord is often
and long absent. Indeed you must tell me
what the water tastes like—
do you drink from tin cups and comb your hair
thirty-two times each night?
From root to end for gloss and shine and oh,
my friend said not to be beloved back
is the only failure. We lay down on the shore
where gulls careen with no such thing
as direction and they had to love us for it.
I trust you when you say the field
unravels in the wheatdust cornhusk shadows.
You know you mustn't linger there.
You must tell me how the land
refuses to enclose you—does it move away from you or
toward you? As it lets you go.

Diagnosis: My Mother's Breast

Recalcitrant, the empire sleeves of her dress hold back
her arms, empty of all long-stemmed flowers now. More blue
enlivens what the wrist keeps track of: the hours
on their daily jaunt around the malls, just as what's ours is wanting
to stay true and earnestly regretting when the sun goes down.
We are pitched into dizziness if we look there, where the *vita* flees.

Her hands are still
behind her back, her mouth is stained with chokeberries.
She flew the coop when the fashion changed. Now our knees
are without hope, too visible for praying on or for the mad
professor to cup his hand around. She wants God sewn

in her hem like a stone in a valance,
like the lead in a bib,
so each time she lifts her dress for a lover He is there
wedged in the balance, accounting
for her breasts, her ribs, and the dress
falling radiant over her head.

Flesh

Wanting to know
is the heart of things, unsaid.
The thing that wants to be known
forgives, but not divinely.
Brokenly, the voice
catches—does it catch water
running, as always, away?
Does it catch the light's
revision on the water,
blue to yellow and its green
return? Has it caught the elbow
of longing, roundly now
turning a corner?
Has it caught the grass?

Visit Home, Summer

The hammock blew, little boat
of ropes in the wind.

Its silken twine through which my wrists
and ankles dangled—

    Once a boy sat cross-legged
in a hammock and we swung. How dark
becomes the grass,

like water our hands
could almost touch.

        Already

dew had beaded the blades.
    That the mind

should be clear of distractions—
    The moon stutters
through the maple leaves.

    How heat condenses
here at night, suspended
while the wind blows the hammock

the wet grass shudders in its wake.

V's Farmhouse

He's at the window now,
at the foot of the bed looking out
to a full blue night the kind the clouds move fast in
and the color's in close as if the sky's right there and you could touch it.
She says she took the screens out, so he opens it
and he's pissing a long arc into the sumac and Queen Anne's lace,
didn't even have to leave the room.
She says he looks majestic
outlined in the window, we see
what we want to see.
To hear is more difficult, this discord
in the pact of things. What he said once before,
turned away from her in the dark
and she, climbing over him to ask so she could hear it.

No one ever died of desire.
They leave the window open
when they sleep, the essential
circumstances fly out: the adulteress
writing a letter, the reprieve
asked for, received
and who it is she loves
already falling past her—she wakes but has only
an opening window, unframed
sky moving faster than anyone could see.

Exchange

You have touched the thing with a needle,
you have hit the nail on the head.

Well, you would if you could. Without a day
being appointed, you arrange

the assignation
and you get there on time. You wait,

cry famine
over a heap of grain. While you're not looking

the grain turns into peacock feathers
you want to touch but can't. Further, if you go

further it will burn. To seek food out of the flame
will get you anywhere. But you must depart

empty-handed to return just the same,
the peacock feather scraggling out of your hair

only as you imagine it, the bread
warm in your hands—

> *Where shall we find the fancy bread,
> in the heart, or in the head?* And the Camembert

you brought there for the rendezvous—gone also
out of your hands. You say you give me

chalk for cheese. Take the chalk. Make use of it.
Go further than the needle,

the eye of the flame.

II Deceptive Country

Okefenokee Swamp

(from Major General G. A. McCall, 1858, described in
The Wild Rivers of North America)

1.

This is deceptive country. Cypress, gum and slash pine
appear to be on land. But we arrived here and they floated:
floating heart and pickerel weed blanket the water so thickly
our canoe seems out of place. If you could see it,
you would think it marks our presence
but cannot explain how we got here at all.

2.

As the sun rose today I looked out upon—what shall I say, the lake?
To my surprise the island I saw yesterday had disappeared.
And the water had receded one hundred yards or so, I'd say.
The island's drifted with the wind,
right past the shore where I was standing.

3.

The pitcher plant is common in the prairies. Green hooded stalks
rise out a foot above the water; insects buzz into their mouths.
Deep within the sheath, Sarah, they alight
on what they take for pollen and they drown
in the pitcher plant's digestive fluids.
This was told to me by someone else. I observe the drowned trees
we've paddled to through dugouts in the narrow channels
which twist through roots and trunks and overhead
the leaves make high noon evening: dark and
darkening.

4.

The swamp in rain sends flows of water to the Suwanee
rising, winding south. The river's slow
and crooked; the sand is gray in shallows.
Tannic acid stains the water when the current's strong.

5.

Came, today, upon that island first seen I cannot say
how long ago. If you could see it, Dear,
you'd know I can't come back. I think of you but cannot leave,
not now, with the heron and egret visible only
in what would be twilight, a blue wing
or white, a shade of difference
in the light,
and then the upstroke, sudden flight, which can be seen
if one is watching, not close
but holding still.

The Hills Have Gone Into the Country

Of the dead. Where everything rises like the color of smoke
and implausible suns. Then they leave. Various trees
take place, take blossom
like nets that catch our ankles in silk holes.

In Rome a priest named Valdimar pronounced my name in Portuguese.
His big brown beard left pockmarks on my collarbone, and his shoes
were dusty. Or they gleamed. I was already gone
into the conditional. What would become

of this our world's ferocity, where shall we lie down to sleep?
The quick fix, the ten-minute nap, our lives that lengthen
like days before solstice renew us
but cannot go whole-hearted into night.

Even the hills hold back a little
of their loveliness, when green is shadowed
rose and blue and we turn our faces toward them
and the light goes down. But we are not

ready, we would still gather pieces of it.

Sunday Afternoon on Kolín Island, 1924-1926

(after the series of photographs by Josef Sudek)

1.

The sidewalk is carved into sections of light
by shadow. The trees embody the human
weakness to lean
halfway out of the picture,
across each other. What three figures are these,
walking steadily into the past?
The third appears to be following
two women, or leading them. *Expose for the shadows.*
The rest will come by itself. Wisteria
flares toward the trees, its flowers all
that caught the flash, that hover over the hedge.

2.

Let us leave this picnic where the women serve potach in aprons
and my small sister sulks on a clod of dirt.
Where shall we hide?
Where are the saplings wide enough
to conceal us, incorporate
us into the bark? We are streaked by the grainy
eye of the camera. It is not that your glasses are fogged.
We are literal, we are looking for something to do.
Our black boots gleam in the sun.

3.

Can you see this space between us,
this aisle of light that reverses our profiles,
our silhouettes? It has been recorded here,
how the suit jacket corners a triangle,
how an elbow angles out. One was saying something,
one was emphatic. The cups on the table are cluttered.
Remind me, when it gets dark, to sweep up the sugar cubes
and eat them whole, here in my starched plaid dress.

4.

There are balloons! There are cigarettes
and pillbox hats. Behind us our heads
cast three shadows. The sloping line from our necks
to our shoulders carves the light into two
mosque facades or inversely, three wavering pillars.
You do not hear the leaves overhead. You do not see the woman
whose hat is pulled rather low over her brow
reach up to swat a fly
and change her mind,
reach for a sugar cube instead. We are all here
where you left us, you who have disappeared
with your clicking shutter, your harbinger light.

Misreading the Adams Memorial

She turned as the sculptor Saint-Gaudens
mouthed her name beneath forsythia: Marian
but she said no, said the stars
turn over like cartwheels reeling. She
stepped out into the garden
while her husband's ink dried in its well.

How she would look when he finished
was a mystery he wanted
to keep, so he covered her
face in drapery, his eyes dazzled
by what hands could see
as shape. And if he envisioned her
body climbed by moss and the green
patina she would become, he quelled it
though she knew, in every early hour she could bear
to be outside (to see him marking
the angle at which her jawbone
curved into her neck) that if his mouth
had bitten there it would remain
obscured.

She would enfold what shapes are
fallings from desire; her throat conveyed her husband's ink
into her veins as if the story could enter her body, as if the time
it took to drink could take her anywhere at all.

Allegory of Air in the Utah Museum of Fine Arts

(after Jan Brueghel, 1568-1625)

She is fleshy, naked, one thigh encircled
by her drapery, red as the cock's comb,
the turkey's wattle.

Her name is Allegory and she hovers.
The air is not her home. Visitor,
she opens her white

body to the dark. If a peacock's tail could
brush her breast with all its eyes enringed
and shimmering, green

yet blue, she would pluck seven feathers to hold
aloft while owls dream, eyes open,
at her feet. Partridge,

ostrich, wanton hen and buzzards black as bats'
wings—true inhabitants and waiting.
Time nicks density:

The air's density where allegory fails
to hold. In her left hand, the earth whirls
like ribbons of gold

in an armillary sphere. A pocketwatch
ticks. How shall the trees stretch further
than the dark? No leaves,

just birds in flight or motionless, and the drop
into earth where the cliff juts out. There,
it lightens. Pine trees

barely visible and mountains. Earth below
the air. And time held in a body
like the wren the moon

cradles in the second-smallest tree.
Or the hummingbird grasped hard by the
angel, who cannot

still her wings. Cognizant of how inheritance
inscribes the fact of grief into his
very signature,

he, the painter, can't look back. Brogans
painted by The Elder have no place
within air, the earth

is not yet lit. The woman's hair is falling,
not dark enough to mark her shadow—
wings of birds, what's missed.

For the Composer of *The Firebird Suite*

Dusk, too, is an open question.

     The sumac trees try to answer, stretching out to catch the sun
         like whiskey seeping into the edges of your bones.

Late June, the nightjars
     fix the last blue light between their wings

     threading it like violin strings, veins
         in which the key of C traverses this whole orchard,
doubles back, and disappears.

     1912, Stravinsky walked the Champs Elysées
after *The Rite of Spring* erupted and the dancers heard nothing
     but the audience raging and their own feet thumping.

I think the trees that lined his walk
     must have quivered like question marks about to be dotted—
the emphatic blot under the undulating line, as if to say the **?** at
                        least, is solid.

All that was historic came after the intermission.
Electricians followed orders
     first to shine the lights, then to cut them. As if the visible

remarks its vanishing under cover of the stage lights,
the spectacle Stravinsky couldn't have
     predicted, couldn't slip back into form.

The orchestra, meanwhile, played on, inaudible
but for brief lulls in *pandemonium*. Everywhere, the dusk peels back

     its pearl grey gloves
         to close its fingers round another day

until the night's unlaced and the cicadas' ceaseless humming frays.

Mary's Angel

If they knelt down in the desert I could tell you
of yellow flowers like sunflowers,
grass tongues flicking their knees.
A man cupped his mouth around my ear
when I was cold and warmed me.
I tell you this because the ocean
is just far enough away for me to want it,
how the soul stirs in her saltwater gown (hem lifting
so the tide can lick her ankles)—you say *she*
for soul; I know only its rustle
and hush like silk, his mouth

on my ear and they have said
he is an angel, as if his tongue could travel down
my collarbone, his mouth to cup my navel,
strong brown legs around his shoulders.
I can imagine wings there. On good days,
I believe him. And why not? His breath tastes fennel.
My feet like blackbread in his hands.
Every hour the sun sinks lower
in its filmy blue glass eye,
like my grandmother's but gashed with orange (the sky's
last gesture and its first), opening,
closing—the soul's throat, her thirst.

Now it changes. He's speaking with care,
wrens' eggs on his tongue. O *strong of heart,*
go where the road leads out of wounds.
He held a compass to my ear: it seemed the ocean roared
and disappeared. Salt brine's brackish
on my hipbones, weight not less
each time we leave. Repetition, how it fills
your mouth, *your mouth,*
that on its ragged beauty I might slake my drought.

Ave Maria

The blizzard drove them home. (*I love to hear the voices merge—*)
Now the thirteenth century, now the choir sang.

If he kissed her
without intent,

without touching,
believe it, they sang in Latin.

Who needs the tattered covenant this body is?
The car glides like an egg through the centuries falling around it,

but the voices merge, singing.
It's 1297. Stone gates,

cobblestone. Where shall we lay our weary heads
if the story holds them together like peas in a pod,

like a hand in a glove: will they ever stop singing,
is there world without end?

Salt streaks the car and a mule deer waits for the lights
to stop blinding. (*It's not that I want to leave—*)

But what they are singing is not about love.
It's about wanting the story, driving all night

and waiting for someone
to say, *that man*

or, *this woman*
is mine.

Expatriate

The sleeves of your coat were too long
for your arms, that time
on the platform made for seeing
someone beginning to drown.
What was it we wanted
to see? What was it
we wanted to hear? The lake
lay still, although the wind
blew softly across.
What we saw was darkened—
a sky of water; the lake, stars.
What we heard was difficult
to catch hold of, not like
a steel fence, a wooden
ladder, but more
like something moving away
(your sleeve, your arm)
in the lissom wind bound for the other shore.

Camera Obscura

Shall we call it indigo, or what-we-almost-had?
To catch the thought, and let it go,
and pull my goose-down collar more tightly around me.
I have left something out: chain-link,
the tear in my sleeve, and my tennis shoe nearly catching.
What could one love more than the close calls?
The rip in the jacket and a crescent feather floating out
to appear in the dark we've now called indigo,
lake-dark. In another jacket and another place
the woodstove burned a hole in my shoulder.
My mother said, don't get attached to *things*.
She patched it with a St. Bernard saying don't eat yellow snow.
Vulgar child, I imagined people saying. My hair hung,
always, over that shoulder.
It (the feather) floats away
for the rest is chaff.
But wait: a tale is introduced and in it,
the friend whom I was with
and have not seen again. The way out of the body, then,
is it forgetting? There is fluidity
of objects at the point of almost remembering.
Almost I can track it, trace it down
the chain-link fence or all across the body
of this water, torn (wherever you are)
not floating (some place
spectacular?), unlinked embodiment of blue.

Requiem

More stars, the night's more starred in Trafalgar Square,
the Romantics gone singing to their deaths. Percy Bysshe,
he made a wish, and the *Don Juan* bore him away. His wrists
in my hair were fluttering things, like birdswings
and he said yes and yes and I believed him.
I played my Italian new guitar. Jane, he said,
Jane. Are we not without recourse,
are the riverbeds full of our bones, the notes
Love takes in her copious hand? Take me
down to the water *whan day is gane and night come in*
an ay the lady followd him, an the tears came hailing down.

So morning bound me to the ordinary.
My coffee clatters in its maker,
gold filtered, darkly ground.
The drowning men went voyaging one moment,
into that love's hands, the sea
that begs to bear you
forward as it fills you
with permission—
O some said yea, and some said nay,
their words did not agree. What peace shall yet be made
with the shoreline and the pelicans
in their shaggy, dun-colored feathers?
They are sitting on a bridge in Florida
where fishermen have gotten used to them.
On my grandfather's bicycle I watch them, and the lights

of the cities are falling. If distances
retain the past, shall we inscribe in them our longing
for the first green star to fix itself nearer than the rest?
A pelican eyes me before lifting off and diving down. The sea
is full of feathers. The rivers are untarrying
to reach its open, salt-laden mouth.

In the Absence of Field Guides

I'd tell of hotels where we slept in wings
under construction, storage rooms
my mother believed in more than reservations.
All the money saved all winter
didn't mean we needed
to know where we would sleep.
The towns were booked: No Vacancy.
Because we read to name things,
to find the picture of the red-tailed hawk
when it holds still over the highway
in a moment you know will come again
but not when; because the unpredictable's a heaven of
its own (how you might drink water from a Mason jar
as if you had been thirsty all your life,
or how my half-excessive rib
cage might fit your hand); because the wings
of hotels filled with sawhorses
are brushing past my face,
there are not birds to try to name. Here
are the linnet's wings, no longer than your hands.

Promiscuity

Tell me the stories of wanting are flowering
past engravings of the poets on the windowsill.
Past the sea that's shoring up its singers:
names and dates of birth and what hurt them
hurtling, now, toward the constant
vow, to listen. And to see
the paper boats go sailing when the body
peels back all its notebooks and its petals.
There are zinnias and anemones afloat.
They can barely hold their perfume in
their veins, they are the story
the earth tells of wanting
to be beautiful, and how it loves
what opens.

Tell me the future
is a border beginning
where the bones of the mind
shine early in the moon's
forsaking light when fullness
is everything and everything is
visible. To be seen is almost as good
as seeing, as the river
says, come in, come in. Tell me
the river.

If radiance can be beheld
then flesh is luminous with seeing.
But to touch is purest knowing
and the wind keening afterward. Both the becoming
and to be leaving. The song of the mind,
the body breathing.
Tell me why one can never be satisfied
though the other is.
Tell me the stories are true.

III Night Skiing

Boneset

He brought her boneset
for her throat, a plant

with dark green leaves and small
white flowers, to crush and make a tea.

He kissed
her throat and small white flowers grew there.

He held
her and her bones became dark green.

He sweetened it with honey and
she drank.

Scavengers

When the racoons came
to the kitchen window, which was open
and through which they stole 2 new
loaves of bread, we wanted
to open it again
and give up our cantaloupe, bananas,
the last green apple
in the blue ceramic bowl.

The creek runs in the moonlight like a narrow escape.
On the rocks the coons had sat
and washed the bread, each bit
of crust torn off and dipped
in the water, turned till every pore soaked through
and the sopping bread was clean enough
to fill their mouths like fish, like bread
washed clean of our hands.

The porchlight swings in the east-going wind
which calls out sometimes in its sleep. If I could be
a body newly risen, washed clean, I'd empty the archives
of white nightgowns hanging from curtain rods all over my room.
One night I woke up and forgot what they were. It was almost
a vision. I would take them down
to the river—a long way?—and send them floating,
boats of dogwood, into darker water
where the roots of trees drink green
wet light and everything returns.

Behind my house the steeples
of Delphinium stay open all night.
Who doesn't know the purple larkspur?
Devil's trumpet, lark's claw, lark's heel—

Wood Heat

The quarter-cord of wood we need for winter
when we heat stones to warm the bed
was buried under snow, and I did not believe
it would be dry enough to burn.
We dug by guessing where to dig, no sign
in three-foot drifts of where the wood had been.
You must know it wasn't cold,
or else it's the meaning of work—when purpose overrides
discomfort and not knowing
if what's buried still will burn.
We found the logs, brushed snow, the bark was dry
though cold. I cannot reason how the wood
resisted its embeddedness in water—you'll say it's frozen,
therefore dry, but still it seems that matter, even water,
should transcend what holds it in, just as the skiers
driving by will see the hollowing we've dug
beside the shed, but not the drifts
that slope down from our windowsills as if a new
geography could shape itself all night and then undo itself
in spite of all its loveliness. This is the cold season.
It's the one I want, the cold that forces us awake
early, when winter rings our names
with frostair breath refutes.

The Sleepless Gardener

The ivy climbs nightly the garden wall
which is made of stones and desires
not to be forsaken. By morning
the ordinary comes to be
itself again: the stone is not aglow
with the moon's light
touch on its surface
and the failure of the first
idea is clear. A wall cannot want
to be beloved by the living
climbing it, a stone can feel
important only to the sleepless
gardener, in bare feet, in the brightening
hour. Night out of the night we are
ourselves gathering what breaks inside of us.

The ivy does not circumvent the stone.
Nor does she live inside of it.
Her hands are cool green implications
of having always somewhere else to go.
Shall the rock's heart lie awake
beating with grief for her indifference?
Why must we want it to? Why when we return
through the screen door to the lit house
hushed with our absence,
will the garden remain the work
of the morning?

There are things that cannot enter
another thing: the world's objects
that make us want to walk out barefoot.
The worlds objects make us want
are never palpable. Underneath
our feet the stones' cold bloom.
The ivy's virescence, the garden wall's.

Seder in Elko

During Passover Seder in Elko,
Nevada, coyotes scatter in the rain.
A Jew in the mountains remembers
a loss that drives the angel inward,
the gust of wind that blows a prophet in.

There goes a tall drink of water, we say,
and he's gone. We keep the glass
half full for him. Out West,
the sun could almost turn to honey on the rocks.
The West is a bare rock

in a bare place despite the woman
who called my office by mistake.
She asked if wildflowers yet were blooming
in the desert. I said this is the School
of Arts & Letters, and that I didn't know.

The world,
an active God in history,
the wandering Nevadan labors to.
She sings without her fingers dipped in water
and the garden yields its good air difficultly.

I love the schist's striations
along the Elko River.
Or the wheeling starred assertions
like *the secret to the latkes is the salt.*
But secrecy is visible out West:
age lines in the rock-face
where some horses used to run
like words out of the desert's
mouth, or dust storms all across Nevada
in which a cry that can't be written

is cursive, and can be heard.

Three-Quarter Moon

And the clouds moving fast in a full blue night.
I'm driving home through Couer d'Alene,
the road like a waltz lurching forward on its one bad knee.

The moon has an elbow, God rocks in its crook.
It's Saturday night. In Seattle, abandoned,
the gasworks rust. Dark roots of the city, how the sky

re-frames them, freezes them
against the bay, against black light like a wing
over an eyelid, or a door coming down

on a cast-iron stove. And all the fire, can it be
so still where steel burned white
like lupine in a grassfire, like the stars going out

in a madwoman's mouth? The fire my friend's hair
was the color of is darker now. He's climbing rusted rungs
hand over hand, he's perched like a nightwatch

over a landscape entered by accident,
no humming, no churning, just hesitant
silence after bone-searing fire.

The canyon road winds its own watch, keeping time's
crooked elbow and the clouds
in the night-blue heart of the night.

The Wild Dogs of Utah

Soon they'll disappear
into the next canyon,
Killyon Canyon,
but we will think of them
as ours—that we called to them
and they listened. We will imagine
they wanted to come but were afraid,
because we do not want,
in the evening light, to be rejected.
We offered them the only thing to give:
our hands tingling as if to stroke the matted fur,
as if everything we touch
will lay its head down in our laps
and will remember how to track our scent,
even when the sage is in full bloom and the madapple
sends its sweet narcotic pollen zigzagging across the cluttered fields.

The Deep Heart's Core is a Suitcase

Or the bed is a pail of water
and cardamom to pour over roses and gold-
flecked paper your knees are wrapped in.
Come to me my plumcake, my heart-of-palm,
the undergrowth grows bright with canaries
and they sing strange songs. What was it when
the angel said? Said give me wine and bread.
For free I will turn your knees to gold. Unwrap them
       from my shoulders where wings are
bent like little doves and the mornings are cold and they hover
under the eaves. Once I threw the sash open (it felt like that—
the sash open) and doves flew off the roof, from over the window
and my heart, too, fluttered. I was in Rome and lost and never in love
in another country. What is American about it?
Bruna cut the sugarcookies into snowflakes and stars.
She trussed a turkey, ironed lace. I couldn't make her believe
I wouldn't miss Thanksgiving,
or that when the boy pulled a knife in the street
he wanted me only to admire it, because it gleamed,
Che bellezza! in its velvet case. Where words are
       perfect, a pail with a hole in the bottom that sinks
into heaven and two brown eyes. There. They remember me better
than Elijah, would-be guest, forgetful of manners,
drinking the wine in a gust of wind
till his throat's stained red. Am I speaking of
memory, its fits and starts, near miss and final plunge
into a drastic, moonlit sea? (But that was in
the Middle West where pilgrims made love in
beds of pine.) Chaste, they called it *bundling*.
They didn't know how fast we hurtle here. And back:
the antique beds under the attic eaves awash with cardamom
and gold flecks from the color *eyes*.

Letter

Let us lie down under the bodies of dark blossoming trees,
the wet bark black from the rain, the blossoms pink or the blossoms
white and their perfume enough to get drunk on from the rain, the rain
        itself having ceased
an hour ago, the rain a prelude to the holiness of the heart's affections
and the good idea of the body's when its bearer lies down
under the petals on the wet black boughs. Ezra,
    there was a night in a make-shift woods
full of mist and the ground a bed of wet brown leaves.
Yes, and such a tree as may be found in such a woods in the Middle West
had fallen ages past and its deeply grooved and grey-black bark a place
against which I did lie. My love held my breast like a bird aflame.

    Those two who wandered there,
past the edge of a hum-drum town, past the last stone silo and the moon-
bright water tower on which nothing was emblazoned
and off which the light of the actual moon reflected blankly—
of them little may be said that has not somewhere once been said before.

    When the sky is deepest blue she thinks of him.
    When the rain-drenched road is black he thinks of her.

It is Spring and the blossoms open and it
rains, briefly, where she lives and it rains,
often, where he lives, and the blossoms
open, and the blossoms open

    Postscript

It is to figures of speech that we return.
My heart is on fire, we say
or, her love rides like the wind.
Do we seek exactitude, or the rain
to sail its ships down our backs? Approximation
or the bridges burning across our paths?

Our shoulders are not stones
to be rounded and rounded by water.
Yet, swimming, I feel smoothed like a surface
that has long been washed by the water; the shoulders
are strongest and lightest there. Shelley, Crane, the sea
     is not a mouth. A lie,
to which we partly acquiesce.
A shell. A hart. A crane
lifting her white wing over the heaving wave
and skimming it with feather's tip: you, there,
with your heart on your sleeve
and the past like a shell in the shape of an ear—
Regard the present: how it is rounded
on earth, in believable weather.

Addendum

Permit me to say the jagged
edges of these mountain-tops
announce the difficulty of view. Bound now
by the Wasatch range, she rides a horse named Keno
into the foothills where the dust is so dry she feels old
even when she leans forward over the horse
and presses gently with her left leg between thigh and knee—
a high, light, momentary signal for cantering,
careening over the sage.
     She remembers Tequila, a horse she rode when she was ten
and later a booze the man she loved could slam
with his head thrown back and his throat exposed strangely like a bird's
breast she once had stroked and felt pulsing.
She doesn't know much about tequila but she thinks it courses like a river
down his strong dark throat. Before that, Tequila was a horse
she rode when she was ten, a horse that veered off the trail
and into the woods, trying to scrape her under
the low-hanging branches, trying to scrape her off.

When the two approached an apple-tree at breakneck speed
she saw the branch too low to lean beneath, to flatten
herself under against the horse's neck. So she, the child, reached her arms
forward and gripped the bough and the horse
kept going while she hung from the branch, legs swinging. All she could see
was the branch coming toward her,
the branch that scraped her palms
when she gripped it, and the trail tilting into miles
of blossoms, of sky as she swung.

Fallings From Us, Vanishings

for Patricia Lee

Tonight the tea steeped strong and honeyed
burst in my mouth like bitter angel.

The sun's streaked in your hair.

Strictly speaking, the night blooms in the desert.
We grow toward error and we take root there.

I would visit untold fragments upon you.

Even the sunflowers' edges are ragged.
They could be rendering outlandish
height or sowing its insouciance.

They could say, all trembling kiss my mouth.

But they would merely be bending
in the hurrying wind.

What shall we do

if the door to the drawing room opens,
Night wraps its fingers in our unbound hair
and we want it to?

Love, there are light years
that Sorrow answers

and her weeping is the sum of what stays.

Night Skiing

I heard coyotes for the first time
in conversation with what moon there was.
I don't know how they knew I was there,
deep in the pines and the junipers,
or whether they knew at all. Accuracy
is all I want—my skis to glide
through Killyon Canyon as if I know
the land and where it dips, where it rises
suddenly beneath the snow and where the creek
is truly frozen.
　　　　How much we know by guessing
and forgetting there are dangers
when you have no light but stars—no way back
if your arms give out or you lose sight
of which trail through which clearing
will take you home again. Wanting nothing
but the sky turned white against the mountains
and the silence not silence but water
running underneath the frozen creek.
　　　　This is how you cross it.
This is how you fall in love
with accuracy. I don't know how much
the body has to do with it, but I would say my lungs
are bruise-colored rivers of trout
cascading faster than Killyon Creek
and with less reason. It is how the story
begins. The mountains lit the sky.
Coyotes devoured the stars.

Versluis Orchards

The birds have stripped a portion
of the corn in the orchard. The woman
who could by marriage be my mother
fills our basket with the ears left most intact.
And Mary Ann, the sister I could have,
around whose head I had wound braids
that mimic something that I crave, is running for the dog;
the dog is running for the pond.

We are there to harvest
what's not riven, what we can
push through to. A palpable
rain, such a finely needled rain,
has threaded the witchgrass yellow.
Late July, the ground will not hold still
with mud that cakes our boots, which I have borrowed.

The woman bends her Dutch-straight body
to share the basket's weight with me.
Her sweatshirt jacket's faded red. On the stalks,
the ears the birds have partly stripped
are for the dogs to scissor down to cob—
at play in these fields that are whose?
Our palms, chafed red around the basket's handles,
shall be not less wounded for the rinsing rain.

Around my hands the braids had fallen,
sixteen years of uncut length each time I tried
to pin them up in coils—too fine,
like cornsilk, too heavy from abundance.
In the yard we dump the corn onto the grass.
The peaches we had placed on top
mark, this day, our need for more
than what must be undone, peeled back, in order
to be made use of. The Harmonies are promises

to sink raw and whole inside our mouths. But first,
they make the corn look greener
for their own midsummer reddened orange.
And before that, we had come
into their portion of the orchard
in time to see them glistening, already ripe
with the rain on their skin and the rain
on our faces like skin.

Bluelight Special

Moreover the rain continues to drive the hollyhocks into the ground.

Coating it white, the Salt Lake advances on shore.
Far beneath the surface, abyssal fish produce light for bait.

In the subway, in Berkeley,

it occurred to me that sumac trees—the threading
    orange of the setting
        sun

going down around the sumac trees
    on a hill, a grassy hill, in Michigan
is enough to cue the couple three seats down from me to kiss.

They believe what they say
and what they see when they say it.

My grandmother walked the beaches every day to look for shells.
At the Osprey County Library she copied lists and saved them
in a shoe box for me: *Scalloped Beauty, American Mussel, Bloody Tooth.*

As if the seashells' names, translated,
could protect her daughter's daughter
    from hurtling forward on a skateboard
in a spray of gravel like rain, the dog's leash wrapped around her wrist.

A man in a pick-up stopped to help me.
He picked the pebbles out of my palms,
unstuck my hair from the blood on my face.

You can almost tell each other stories
of what the light is like in another town.

You can almost see the gravel-scars
        marking the body in the visible world

and the universe having a sale
on the marked-down, the seasonal or nearly

perfect things missing directions.